JUNGLE
ADVENTURES
By Katy Lennon

Series Editor Deborah Lock
Project Editor Camilla Gersh
Editors Caryn Jenner, Katy Lennon, Pomona Zaheer
Project Art Editor Hoa Luc
Design Assistant Emma Hobson
Art Editor Yamini Panwar
US Senior Editor Shannon Beatty
Producer, Pre-Production Francesca Wardell
Illustrator Hoa Luc
DTP Designers Anita Yadav, Vijay Kandwal
Picture Researcher Sakshi Saluja
Managing Editor Soma B. Chowdhury
Managing Art Editor Ahlawat Gunjan

Reading Consultant
Linda B. Gambrell, Ph.D.
Subject Consultant
David Emmett, Conservation International

With special thanks to Amy van Nice,
Wildlife Alliance

First American Edition, 2015

Published in the United States by
DK Publishing
345 Hudson Street
New York, New York 10014

15 16 17 18 19 10 9 8 7 6 5 4 3 2 1

001—273355—April/15

Published in Great Britain by Dorling Kindersley Limited.

A catalog record for this book is available from the Library of Congress.

ISBN: 978-1-4654-2931-5 (pb)
ISBN: 978-1-4654-2930-8 (hc)

Printed and bound in China

DK books are available at special discounts when purchased in bulk for sales promotions, premiums, fund-raising, or educational use. For details, contact: DK Publishing Special Markets, 345 Hudson Street, New York, New York 10014 or SpecialSales@dk.com.

The publisher would like to thank the following for their kind permission to reproduce their photographs:
(Key: a-above; b-below/bottom; c-center; f-far; l-left; r-right; t-top)

1 **Alamy Images**: Daniel Santacatalina Laborda. 6–7 **Dreamstime.com**: Pixelalex. 8–9 **Corbis**: Yi Lu/Viewstock. 11 **Getty Images**: webphotographeer/E+. 13 **Alamy Images**: Alexey Gnilenkov. 14 **Getty Images**: Mark Carwardine/Photolibrary. 16 **Alamy Images**: Gustav Gonget/G&B Images. 20 **Dorling Kindersley**: Jamie Marshall (bc). 20–21 **Dorling Kindersley**: Bethany Dawn. 21 **Dorling Kindersley**: Tim Draper/Rough Guides (tl); Bethany Dawn (cb).23 **Alamy Images**: mediacolor's. 25 **Alamy Images**: Ginette Peach. 29 **Alamy Images**: Paul Kingsley. 31 David Emmett, Conservation International: (t, br). 35 **Corbis**: 145/Don Farrall/Ocean (bl). 36–37 **Dreamstime.com**: Lightzoom (b). 43 David Emmett, Conservation International. 45 **Getty Images**: Danita Delimont/Gallo Images. 47 **Alamy Images**: Pawel Bienkowski. 49 **Alamy Images**: Terry Whittaker. 50 **Getty Images**: Peter Charlesworth / LightRocket. 52 **Alamy Images**: Sam Yue (l). 54 **Dreamstime.com**: Irochka (cl); Andrey Sukhachev (br). 55 **Dreamstime.com**: Dannyphoto80 (br); Peter Wollinga (cl). 56 **Alamy Images**: Bill Attwell (bl); McDonald/Steve Bloom Images (cl). 57 **Alamy Images**: Ganesh H Shankar (tl); Henry Westheim Photography (bl). **Dorling Kindersley**: Whipsnade Zoo, Bedfordshire (crb). 58 **Alamy Images**: Anders Blomqvist. 59 David Emmett, Conservation International. 60 David Emmett, Conservation International: (bl, br). 61 David Emmett, Conservation International: (clb, br). 62 **Alamy Images**: Kjersti Joergensen. 64 **Alamy Images**: Wayne Neal. 67 **Getty Images**: Ricardo Reitmeyer/E+. 68–69 **Alamy Images**: Atlaspix. 70 **Corbis**: 13/Martin Harvey/Ocean (br). 71 **Corbis**: Shin Yoshino/Minden Pictures (tr). 72 **Alamy Images**: Gary Jecan/Danita Delimont, Agent (cl); blickwinkel/Layer (cra); komkrit tonusin (crb). 73 **Alamy Images**: Peter Newton (tl). **Getty Images**: Paul Kennedy/Lonely Planet Images (cl). naturepl.com: Nick Garbutt (cr). 75 **Getty Images**: Caroline Schiff/The Image Bank. 76 **Alamy Images**: Daniel Santacatalina Laborda (l). 78 **Alamy Images**: Michael Stubblefield. 81 David Emmett, Conservation International. 82 Koulang Chey, Conservation International. 83 David Emmett, Conservation International. 86–87 **Alamy Images**: Tim Gainey. 87 David Emmett, Conservation International: (br). 88 David Emmett, Conservation International. 90–91 **Alamy Images**: David Davis Photoproductions RF. 92–93 **Alamy Images**: Thailand Wildlife. 95 **Alamy Images**: Zoonar/Vladimir Blinov. 98–99 David Emmett, Conservation International. 101 **Alamy Images**: Bradley Ireland/Danita Delimont, Agent. 103 **Alamy Images**: ZUMA Press, Inc.. 104–105 **Getty Images**: Steve Winter/National Geographic. 106 **Alamy Images**: dpa picture alliance archive. 108 **Corbis**: ZSSD/Minden Pictures. 112–113 **Alamy Images**: Pawel Bienkowski. 112 Wildlife Alliance: Amy Van (c). 113 **Alamy Images**: Terry Whittaker (cla, cl, cr, crb).115 **Dreamstime.com**: Jiripravda (tl); Riyanto Samui Daja (br).
Jacket images: Front: Getty Images: Tom Brakefield; **Back: Corbis**: Yi Lu/Viewstock (t); **Spine: David Emmett, Conservation International** (b).

All other images © Dorling Kindersley
For further information see: www.dkimages.com

A WORLD OF IDEAS:
SEE ALL THERE IS TO KNOW

Contents

Location

Deep in the humid mountain forests of Cambodia lies a mysterious world filled with rare and undiscovered animals. Many scientists travel here in the hope of discovering the secrets of the Cardamom Mountains.

Cambodia

■ Siem Reap

Mekong River

▲ Cardamom Mountains

Phnom Penh

Prek Tnort River

Koh Kong

outheast Asia

Aman Sea

Gulf of
Thailand

Expedition Team

The deepest forests of the Cardamom Mountains are a place where few hu venture. Those who are brave enou go are often specialists in a certain f Here are a few of the scientists yo expect to find in the jungle.

MAMMALOGIST
mammal expert

ORNITH
bird e

HERPETOLOGIST
reptile and
amphibian expert

ECOLOGI
studies how animals
with the environn

Southeast Asia

Andaman Sea

Gulf of
Thailand

Expedition Team

The deepest forests of the Cardamom Mountains are a place where few humans venture. Those who are brave enough to go are often specialists in a certain field. Here are a few of the scientists you could expect to find in the jungle.

MAMMALOGIST
mammal expert

ORNITHOLOGIST
bird expert

HERPETOLOGIST
reptile and amphibian expert

ECOLOGIST
studies how animals interact with the environment

ICHTHYOLOGIST

fish expert

ENTOMOLOGIST

insect expert

ARACHNOLOGIST

spider expert

BOTANIST

plant expert

ZOOLOGIST

studies the evolution, distribution, and habits of animals

CHAPTER 1
Welcome to the Jungle

From the tops of mountains to the bottom of the ocean, our Earth has many unexplored areas. Intrepid explorers have spent years traveling the globe, but still they have only just scratched the surface.

Today, many scientists fight against the wind, rain, and scorching sun in the most unwelcoming climates to try to understand our planet and the creatures that live on it. One area that has a wealth of wildlife to study is the Cardamom Mountains in Cambodia.

Half of all the world's species live in jungles and the Cardamom Mountains offer a great expanse that is teeming with wildlife. From big cats and elephants to plants, fish, birds, and insects the jungle is a treasure trove for any budding scientist.

The Cardamom Mountains has been left largely untouched until recent years. It is the perfect place to make new and exciting discoveries by studying wildlife in its natural habitat.

Scientists who conduct their research in the wild rather than in a laboratory are called field scientists.

Not just anyone can become a field scientist—as well as having an interest in wildlife they also need to be patient, have a keen eye for detail, and most importantly, be brave! Field scientists will often spend months at a time sleeping in tents, eating canned food, and keeping one eye open for dangerous animals. Living in these conditions isn't for everyone, but a passion for nature and a desire for discovery is what helps keep field scientists eager—even if they happen to find a sneaky critter camping out in their sleeping bag!

Living and working in the jungle is no easy feat and it requires a lot of preparation. Before their expedition, scientists will research the area that they are visiting and plan their experiments. They will collect supplies and practice survival techniques to make sure that they are ready for anything. Scientists traveling to the jungle also need injections to protect them from dangerous diseases, such as malaria and dengue fever, which are carried by mosquitoes.

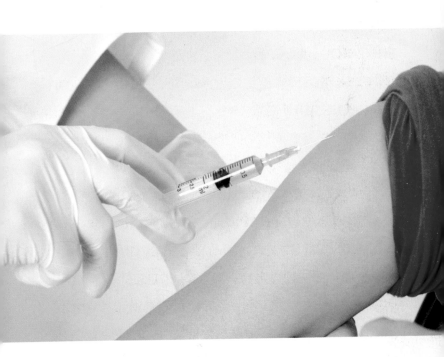

Research that is carried out in places such as the Cardamom Mountains can answer many questions about life on Earth. Scientists conduct experiments to try and understand how animals and plants survive in the wild, for example: which animals eat certain plants; how many species of frog are in the Cambodian jungle; or why some crocodiles are in danger of extinction.

Thanks to previous brave explorers, scientists know where to look for specific animals and plants. However, it is the excitement of the unknown and the possibility of discovery that drives them ever farther into the jungle.

Located in southwest Cambodia, the Cardamom region is an astounding 2.5 million acres. The mountain range is an area of outstanding natural beauty and the highest point in Cambodia, Mount Aural, which stands at 5,946 feet, is situated there. In addition to the jungle, the area also

provides homes for many water-dwelling creatures. There are five main rivers that run through the mountains. One of these rivers is the Mekong River, a substantial, winding waterway and the longest river in Southeast Asia.

In order to collect useful results from their experiments, scientists have a lot of specialized equipment and technology available to them.

One such gadget is a camera trap (pictured above). This can be set up in the jungle and left to capture images of the wildlife. The camera has a motion sensor so that it will take a picture when a creature passes in front of its lens. In this way, scientists can observe animals acting naturally—the presence of humans might spook them and scare them away.

One type of survey that scientists undertake in the Cardamoms is a biodiversity survey. This is when scientists count how many different types of animals they can see and how many there are of each type. By monitoring these numbers, scientists can figure out if any animals are in danger. Some species have become less common in the Cardamom Mountains, which indicates that they may be under threat of becoming endangered. Once scientists learn which animals are in trouble, they can try and find a way to help them.

Why are camera traps useful to scientists?

In their quest for knowledge, scientists often have to venture far off the beaten track. This means that they need to use alternative modes of transportation to reach the far flung corners of the jungle.

To get to the Cardamom Mountains, explorers can fly into Phnom Penh, the capital city of Cambodia. They will then be able to drive to the outskirts of the mountains. However, from this point onward, their trip will become a lot more treacherous.

The roads begin to disappear the nearer they get to the jungle and scientists have to

rely on helicopters to get them closer to their camp. Flying in a helicopter is the easiest and quickest way to get from place to place in the jungle, so it does help if scientists are not afraid of heights.

Once they touch down in the jungle, explorers will have to hike to their campsite and research station. Teams of explorers will often have a guide to help them navigate through the dense jungle. When the foliage is too thick to walk through, they will cut down the plants using a machete.

Hiking through the jungle is thirsty work and explorers need to be fit and healthy. What looks like a small distance on a map can often take hours of hiking. Once they reach their destination, the explorers can start to set up their camp and get ready for their jungle adventure.

Camping Gear Checklist

You will need lots of equipment if you are going to spend a long time in the jungle. Don't leave home without this essential gear.

CHECKLIST

- [x] A first aid kit is vital for any cuts, scrapes, or illness. Make sure none of the medicine is out of date.

- [x] A wash kit will have small bottles of soap, shampoo, hand sanitizer, and anything else you need.

- [x] A clothes-washing kit should contain a collapsible bowl, detergent, and gloves.

- [x] A compass will help you find your way.

- [x] Waterproof bags have infinite uses but are especially handy for keeping clothes dry and for storing dirty clothes.

- [x] Clotheslines are essential for hanging your clothes out to dry.

- [x] A pocketknife can be used for lots of small jobs, from cutting rope to extracting fishhooks.

WITH A BACKPACK, ORGANIZATION AND EASY ACCESS ARE KEY. USE THESE BASIC PACKING TIPS AS A GUIDE.

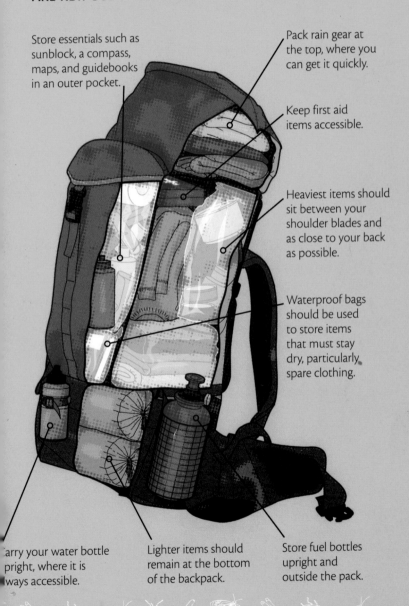

Store essentials such as sunblock, a compass, maps, and guidebooks in an outer pocket.

Pack rain gear at the top, where you can get it quickly.

Keep first aid items accessible.

Heaviest items should sit between your shoulder blades and as close to your back as possible.

Waterproof bags should be used to store items that must stay dry, particularly spare clothing.

Carry your water bottle upright, where it is always accessible.

Lighter items should remain at the bottom of the backpack.

Store fuel bottles upright and outside the pack.

Naga Tours

Allow yourself to be transported back to an enchanting and mysterious ancient world with Naga Tours. Our three-day Angkor itinerary will guide you through the dense jungle to the ancient capital of the great Khmer Empire.

CAMBODIA

DAY 1: Angkor Wat

Begin with a visit to Angkor Wat at sunrise. The largest religious monument in the world, "Angkor Wat" literally means "the City that is a Temple." Built during the 12th century by King Suryavarman II, this spectacular complex was originally dedicated to the Hindu god Vishnu. It became a Buddhist sanctuary in the 13th century.

DAY 2: Angkor Thom and the Bayon

Spend your second day at the ancient Khmer city of Angkor Thom, which means "Great City." Founded by King Jayavarman VII in the late 12th century, it was the largest city in the Khmer Empire at one time. The most famous site in Angkor Thom is the Bayon, a temple with more than 200 huge stone faces.

DAY 3: Ta Prohm

Finish your tour by taking in the spectacular Ta Prohm. Perhaps best known as the temple from *Tomb Raider*, it was a Buddhist monastery built during the reign of King Jayavarman II. Now covered with the sprawling roots of giant banyan trees, it may be the most mysterious of all the temples at Angkor.

CHAPTER 2
Setting up Camp

Many tribes live in jungle environments around the world. Their way of life is simple and they rely on the trees around them for food, drink, shelter, and clothing. There is no shortage of building material and huts can be made using tree trunks, leaves, and any other flora that can be found in the jungle.

This way of life is normal to many people, but it can be a shock for some scientists who are used to more modern living conditions. Many jungle camps only have basic amenities but they can be surprisingly homelike. Camps will often have cabins with kitchens, laboratories, and even real toilets!

The Cardamom Mountains receive 150–190 inches of rainfall a year, so the wooden cabins that scientists sleep in need to be waterproof. They have sloping roofs

so that water can easily run off them and are built on tall stilts. Keeping the cabin raised above the jungle floor means that it keeps it drier and equipment can be stored underneath. The tall stilts also help prevent unwelcome jungle critters from sneaking inside to escape the rain.

Although the comfort of base camp does seem inviting, once the real work starts scientists have to head deeper into the jungle. Carrying all the supplies they need, jungle explorers hike farther into the trees and farther away from human civilization.

Once they have reached a suitable place to conduct their experiments, explorers set up some slightly less cozy sleeping compartments. These areas will consist of: a hammock; a canvas covering called a fly; and a mosquito net.

Installing the fly first, each end should be tied between two sturdy trees. This will be the top layer that keeps the rain off the person below. Next, the hammock should be tied underneath the fly with the mosquito net hung above. This net will stop any little bloodsucking insects from getting inside. This type of shelter is called a bivouac, or bivvy for short.

A great jungle tip is to make sure that

nothing is left on the ground—the jungle dew will make it soaking wet, or some jungle critters might tuck inside for a nap.

Nights in the jungle are cold because of the dense tree canopy. Explorers have to make sure that they are wrapped up as snug as a bug to get a good night's sleep and prepare themselves for the exciting discoveries that lie ahead.

Mealtime in the Cambodian jungle might not be a gourmet feast but there are many delicious and exotic delights available. The jungle is rich in nutrients for those who know where to find it. Fresh fruit such as finger bananas, mangosteen, and rambutans are in abundance and can offer a welcome change to the canned sardines and oat crackers that explorers carry in their packs.

Foraging for fruit can be dangerous and should be left to the experts. A few rules that can help an explorer find food that is safe to eat are: avoid plants with white or yellow berries; don't eat mushrooms; and avoid plants with thorns.

Staying hydrated is a vital part of survival in the jungle. The intense humidity and hard physical labor means that explorers sweat more than usual. They therefore need to make sure that they drink lots of water so that they don't become dehydrated. There is a large quantity of water in the jungle but most of it is not fit to drink. Water can carry parasites and bacteria that will make humans very sick. However, hardened explorers with proper survival training know exactly how to combat this. Passing water through a filter or boiling it over a fire removes or kills any organisms living within it, making it safe to drink. Exploring is thirsty work so keeping all team members fed and watered is of high priority for any expedition.

If the poisonous food and unsafe drinking water isn't enough to put you off the jungle life altogether, there are plenty of other dangers to give you the creeps. Mosquitoes, snakes, spiders, and beetles all scurry and flit around in the hazy jungle heat, looking for their next meal. Scientists and explorers can also fall prey to another type of bloodsucker—leeches!

In the tall, damp jungle grass these black, slippery worms lie in wait to attach their suckers to any warm-blooded animal that passes through their territory. Although not deadly, leeches can give their victim quite a shock. Leeches attach themselves to the skin using a sucker in their mouth. They release a substance that makes blood flow more quickly when they are drinking and then let out another chemical that slows the flow when they're finished.

If a leech is ripped off before it has finished feeding, the wound will bleed more than normal. The best thing to do is wait for it to have its fill, then it will simply drop off and continue on its way.

Despite its dangers, the jungle is a beautiful place for scientists to work. However, with excitement around every corner, staying safe is always important. Trips, falls, cuts, and bites can be more serious in the jungle and so exploration teams always need to have help on standby.

If a team member falls ill or becomes injured, they may need urgent medical attention. The quickest way for them to get help is to be airlifted out of the jungle by helicopter.

Jungle trees are packed tightly together, making it difficult for helicopters to land. When a person needs to be evacuated, a helicopter hovers over the jungle canopy and a medic abseils down to the jungle floor. If the patient needs to be taken to the hospital, a stretcher is lowered down and the person is strapped securely to it.

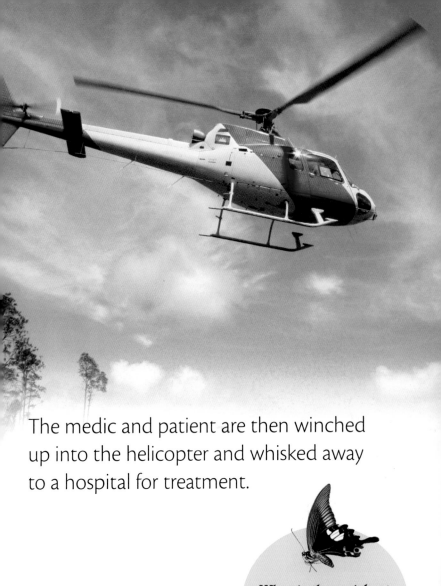

The medic and patient are then winched up into the helicopter and whisked away to a hospital for treatment.

What is the quickest way out of the jungle?

Getting Ready for Bed

If you have to spend the night out in the jungle, a fly-and-hammock combination is the best type of shelter. This arrangement will provide plenty of ventilation and keep you dry. Here is how to set it up.

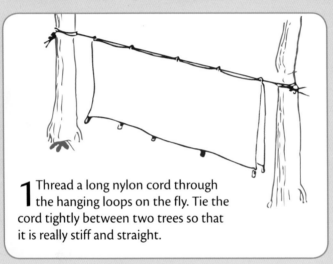

1 Thread a long nylon cord through the hanging loops on the fly. Tie the cord tightly between two trees so that it is really stiff and straight.

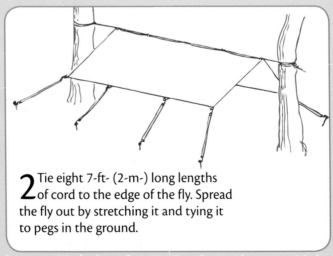

2 Tie eight 7-ft- (2-m-) long lengths of cord to the edge of the fly. Spread the fly out by stretching it and tying it to pegs in the ground.

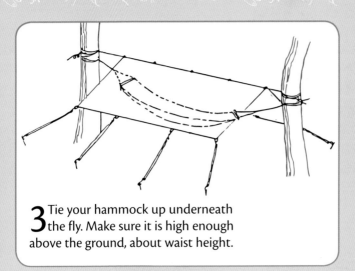

3 Tie your hammock up underneath the fly. Make sure it is high enough above the ground, about waist height.

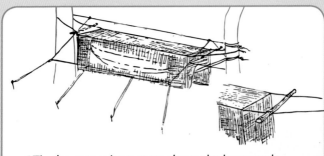

4 Tie the mosquito net up above the hammock and below the fly. Fit a thin, 3-ft (1-m) stick onto the net on either side to create a box shape. Tuck the mosquito net into the hammock to create a totally enclosed space.

NOW GET INTO THE HAMMOCK, BUT TRY NOT TO FALL OUT THE OTHER SIDE!

How to Avoid Bites and Stings

The most dangerous animals are not tigers, bears, or crocodiles; they are much smaller creatures that bite, sting, or transmit nasty diseases. You will need to know how to avoid these—and what to do if you are hurt!

MOSQUITOES

The Dangers

Millions of people suffer from diseases carried by tropical mosquitoes. These include yellow fever, West Nile virus, dengue fever, and malaria.

What to do:

- use insect repellent on your skin
- always sleep under a mosquito net
- use mosquito-repellent candles and other devices.

ANTS

The Dangers

Many ants live in large colonies, which they defend by swarming over intruders and biting or stinging them.

What to do:

- stay away from nests
- get medical help fast if you suffer multiple stings or if any of the stings are inside your nose, mouth, or throat.

SNAKES

The Dangers

Most snakes are not venomous at all, but some can be deadly. Cambodia has many venomous snakes, including cobras and vipers.

What to do:

- wear sturdy boots
- use a stick to tap the ground in front of you to ward off snakes
- if someone is bitten, seek medical help immediately and keep the affected area below the level of the victim's heart.

SPIDERS

The Dangers

Nearly all spiders are venomous. Luckily, very few are able to bite humans, but some spiders are very dangerous. There are many venomous spiders in Cambodia.

What to do:

- avoid places where spiders might live
- carefully check clothing and footwear
- if you are bitten by a spider, immediately seek medical attention.

Other Dangers

Avoid ticks by wearing long pants and sturdy boots.

Check clothes and footwear carefully to avoid scorpions.

Fruits of Cambodia

Visit a Cambodian market, and you will be able to experience a range of exotic and delicious fruits. They are excellent in salads or alone as a snack.

DURIAN
Sweet, rich, and smelly

MANGOSTEEN
Juicy and mildly scented

DRAGON FRUIT
Mildly sweet and grainy

CUSTARD APPLES
Sweet, grainy, and fragrant

ASIAN BANANAS
Tiny, flavorful, and creamy

PINEAPPLE
Tangy and refreshing

GREEN COCONUT
Rubbery and sweet

GUAVA
Sweet, tart, and juicy

RAMBUTANS
Mild, juicy, and sweet

PAPAYA
Smooth and fragrant

37

Rescue Helicopter

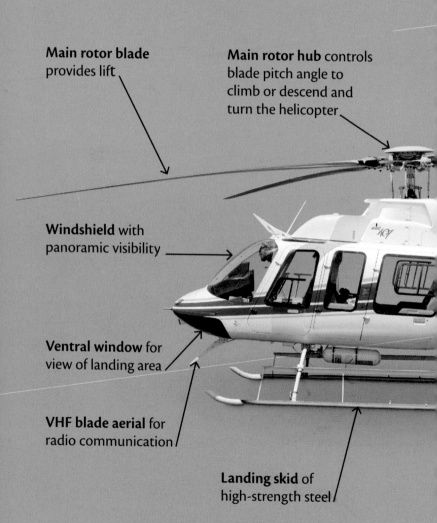

Main rotor blade provides lift

Main rotor hub controls blade pitch angle to climb or descend and turn the helicopter

Windshield with panoramic visibility

Ventral window for view of landing area

VHF blade aerial for radio communication

Landing skid of high-strength steel

Helicopters are very useful for scientists going on expeditions to remote areas. Here is a type of helicopter that is often used in search and rescue operations and medical evacuations.

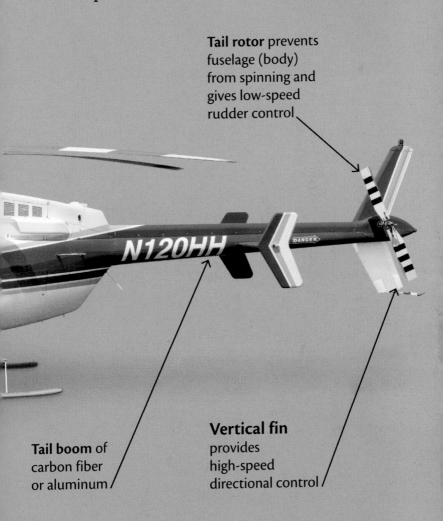

Tail rotor prevents fuselage (body) from spinning and gives low-speed rudder control

Tail boom of carbon fiber or aluminum

Vertical fin provides high-speed directional control

Helicopter Hand Signals

Helicopters make too much noise for their pilots to be able to hear instructions from people on the ground. Instead, they rely on hand signals such as these.

I AM YOUR SIGNALING GUIDE

START ENGINE

HOVER FACING ME

LOWER A LITTLE

UP A LITTLE

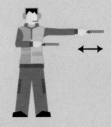

MOVE RIGHT

MOVE LEFT

TAKE OFF

LAND

STOP ENGINES

CHAPTER 3
Life in the Jungle

The wide range of plants and animals living in the Cardamom Mountains is largely due to the type of climate that the area has. Cambodia has two seasons—the dry season and the wet season. The dry season runs from October to April and blasts the country with dry winds, dust, and scorching temperatures. May to September brings heavy rainfall, allowing plants to rejuvenate and absorb some much needed moisture.

The monsoon rains that the mountains experience have enabled the jungle trees to grow to fantastic heights. The canopy can reach up to 150 feet—a dizzy height for any tree-dwelling creature. There are also patches of grassland. Here the grass can reach up to 4 feet tall, providing the perfect hiding place for many prowling animals.

The Cardamom region is thought to be home to more than 600 species of birds, mammals, amphibians, and reptiles, and countless species of insects. These creatures have all adapted to survive in the warm and wet conditions that the area offers.

When an exploration team flies over the jungle in a helicopter they will be able to see a scattering of tall, thin trees that shoot up and away from the jungle—this is called the emergent layer. Just below them is the next layer of trees, peeping their heads up past their neighbors' in a bid for sunlight. This next layer is called the canopy.

The forest canopy forms a leafy roof, shielding the ground and absorbing most of the sunlight. Many animals have adapted to life in the treetops and the canopy is an area brimming with creatures. Much of this wildlife remains hidden to those on the ground and some creatures rarely, if ever, descend to the forest floor.

The canopy layer offers animals protection from predators down on the forest floor because many of the bigger animals have not adapted to be able to climb high up into the trees. In order for tree-dwellers to enjoy their lofty lifestyle, they need to be able to cling tightly to the tree branches. Many animals have strong tails, flexible bodies, or sticky toes, to keep them from falling into the path of the hungry predators waiting below.

If you delve deeper into the jungle, you will find the understory layer. This part of the jungle, just above the ground, is dark and damp. The plants that grow in the hot, sticky air do not require much light. Their large leaves snatch every spot of sunlight that pierces the canopy, and many animals scuttle around in their shade.

Long ropelike vines wind up the trunks of the trees and loop between their branches. These offer a handy bridge for the jungle's tightrope-walking creatures to use. However, they must be careful—snakes and vines can look dangerously similar and they wouldn't want to grab onto the tail of an angry serpent!

Some animals thrive in the darkness of the jungle, but others long for sunnier places. These creatures tend to favor the patches of grassland that are dotted

throughout the jungle. These areas offer the perfect place to enjoy an afternoon, basking in the Cambodian heat.

For animals that can't jump, fly, or climb, the forest floor is the part of the jungle that they call "home." Many small plants, such as ferns, mosses, and fungi grow in the dim and damp conditions, and the strong roots of the trees above are anchored here.

The dead leaves that flutter down from the treetops provide nutrients for the floor-dwelling creatures below. Worms, beetles, and termites are among the insects that feed on this plant debris—they are part of a group of animals called "decomposers."

Decomposers recycle jungle waste and release it back into the soil. Plants then feed on this nutrient-rich earth. The jungle life cycle shows that even the tiniest animals are very important. All plants and creatures in the jungle depend on each other, and if even one of them dies out, it can have great, and even dire, consequences for the others.

The jungle has more habitats than any other environment on the planet because

of its warm and stable climate. To find all of these different areas, scientists not only need to search up toward the canopy, but also along the ground and into the water.

Of the many habitats in the Cardamom Mountains, the rivers are the most important. Not only are they home to many fish, reptiles, and amphibians, but they also provide drinking water for all other animals in the jungle and for approximately one third of Cambodia's human population.

The monsoon rains fall heaviest on the Cardamom Mountains plateau—an area of flat, high ground. This provides the source, or starting point, for many of the country's rivers.

These life-giving waterways slither through the country and provide water for fish farms and rice paddies. These in turn give people a source of food and money.

All habitats have a delicate balance of life, and all the plants and creatures within it are dependent on each other. From river weeds and algae, to fish and crocodiles, everything needs to eat, and the rivers provide plenty of nourishment to go around.

Rivers have a continuous flow of water that runs in one direction—from the source to the mouth (where it meets the sea). All plants and animals that live in this environment need to be able to contend with this movement of water to avoid getting swept away. Many have adapted and can cling to rocks, hide from the current, or swim against it.

Cardamom

November 22, 2002

NEW SNAKE SPECIES DISCOVERED IN CARDAMOM MOUNTAINS

By Ally LeCroc, Science Editor

RARE WOLF SNAKE FOUND IN CARDAMOMS.

A species of wolf snake has been recorded for the first time in the Cardamom Mountains, according to findings to be published in the December issue of *Herpetologica* magazine.

Wolf snakes are nonvenomous and are identified by their wolflike teeth, where most other snakes have fangs.

Courier

Herpetologists Jennifer C. Daltry and Wolfgang Wüster first discovered the unusual snake on a boulder near a forest stream while conducting a survey of the wildlife in the Cardamom Mountains in the year 2000.

They have named it *Lycodon cardamomensis*, or the Cardamom Mountains wolf snake.

Daltry and Wüster explained that, although they had found only one specimen, its unique characteristics convinced them that it must be a new species. The Cardamom Mountains wolf snake has a distinctive pattern of six well-defined, broad white bands across the tail and six across the black body.

Until recently, the region was relatively unexplored, but the lush forests of the Cardamom Mountains are now gradually being depleted by logging and slash-and-burn farming. As a result, the Cardamom Mountains wolf snake will be included on the Red List of Threatened Species by the International Union for the Conservation of Nature (IUCN).

A concentrated effort to survey the biodiversity of the Greater Mekong region—of which the Cardamom Mountains is a part—is under way.

Fellow conservationist Dr. David Emmett said of the find, "This is an exciting discovery, and it's only the beginning. New species are being discovered here all the time, but it's a race against time to document all of the species and ensure that they are protected before they are lost forever."

Taxonomy of Living Things

To help us understand how life forms on the planet are related to one another, scientists organize them into six large groups called kingdoms. This classification is called taxonomy.

PLANTS

Plants are complex, multicelled organisms that can make their own food. They include mosses, conifers, and flowering plants.

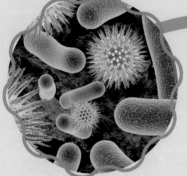

EUBACTERIA

These are simple, single-celled bacteria. This type of bacteria can cause diseases or turn milk into yogurt.

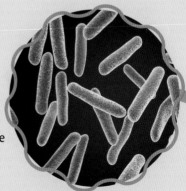

ARCHAEOBACTERIA

These simple, single-celled bacteria are thought to be among the oldest living things on the planet. They can survive in hostile environments such as boiling water.

SPLITTING UP THE SPECIES

Kingdoms are very broad groups, so scientists split them up into smaller and smaller groups. Scientists divide each group according to how similar or different the members are. The classification for a tiger looks like this:

KINGDOM	PHYLUM	CLASS	ORDER	FAMILY	GENUS	SPECIES
Animalia (animals)	Chordata (chordates)	Mammalia (mammals)	Canivora (carnivores)	Felidae (cats)	Panthera (big cats)	Tigris (tiger)

ANIMALS

Animals range from the very simple, such as a sponge, to the highly complex, such as mammals and humans.

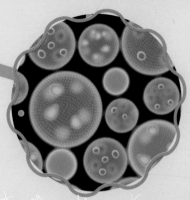

FUNGI

Mushrooms, molds, and yeasts are all fungi. Fungi gain their energy by breaking down dead plants and animals.

PROTISTS

Protists include amoebae, slime molds, algae, and protozoa. They are microscopic single-celled organisms, and each species is different.

Animals of the Cardamom Mountains

Asian elephant

Asian elephants have smaller ears than African elephants and have had a close relationship with humans for thousands of years.

Flying squirrel

These squirrels come out at night and can extend their arms and legs to create a parachute with their bodies.

Clouded leopard

Clouded leopards are the smallest of the big cats. They are excellent at climbing trees, and their markings are perfect camouflage in the forest.

Great hornbill

This bird is the largest member of
the hornbill family and is named
for its huge yellow bill.

100 in./250 cm

80 in./200 cm

Malayan sun bear

This small bear uses its teeth
and extremely long, curved
claws to climb trees.

60 in./150 cm

Siamese crocodile

Long thought to have
become extinct in the
Cardamom Mountains,
the Siamese crocodile
was rediscovered in 2000.

40 in./100 cm

20 in./50 cm

0 in./0 cm

CHAPTER 4
Magnificent Mammals

Animals of all shapes and sizes live in the Cambodian jungle, among them is a certain group defined as mammals. Mammals are warm-blooded creatures who usually have a layer of fur on their skin. Some examples of mammals include tiny shrews, prowling tigers, and lumbering elephants.

Scientists who specialize in the study of mammals are called mammalogists.

Some mammals are very good at hiding in the jungle trees and can be difficult to spot, even for an expert. Mammals, such as tigers, are endangered, which means that there are very few of them in the wild. When trying to spot tigers in Cambodia, scientists might have to lie in wait for hours, or even days, to catch even a quick glimpse of the crafty cats.

Patience is a virtue, as the saying goes, and mammalogists need to have it in large amounts. Many mammals only venture out into the open at nighttime, making them difficult to track, but scientists have a few tricks to help find them. They can set up camera traps to take pictures like the ones below, which show: a serow; an Asian golden cat; a family of porcupines; and a sambar deer snuffling through the jungle.

Mammalogists can also track and tag mammals. This helps them keep a record of the ones they have seen. It is often quite difficult to tell one porcupine from another, so giving them a numbered tag helps identify individuals.

In an area such as the Cardamoms, which doesn't have many human visitors, scientists have to try their best not to disturb the animals or their environment. Small mammals need to be handled with care and after they have been caught, examined, and their details logged, need to be released back into the wild, unharmed. Large animals also need to be approached with extreme caution. It is always useful to remember that animals are usually more scared of you than you are of them.

Monkeys and apes belong to a family of mammals called primates and are close relatives of humans. As expert climbers, monkeys are adapted to spend their time swinging in the trees. Monkeys have strong tails and flexible hands that help them move around with ease. Although some apes also live in trees, they are different from monkeys because they do not have tails. Primates can jump from tree to tree and land with astounding precision thanks to their forward-facing eyes, which help them judge the distance between branches. Primates have a healthy diet of fruit and leaves that they gather from the treetops during their daily jungle acrobatics.

Primates live in jungles all over the world, and in the Cardamom Mountains, scientists can expect to find many different types of monkeys, gibbons, and macaques. Gibbons are sometimes referred to as lesser apes and are the smallest members of the ape family. They are territorial animals and guard their space and food in the jungle by making whooping calls at dawn and dusk. These warnings are ear-splittingly loud and can be heard up to one mile away.

Monkeys and apes are incredibly clever mammals who are quick to learn and are curious about their surroundings. They have learned how to use tools such as twigs and stones to get food out of tight places and crack open nuts.

Alongside the loud and boisterous mammals in the jungle, there are those who live a more serene and quiet lifestyle. Deer are shy creatures that are often hunted by other animals—so they need to be wary of strangers. Deer are the only animals that have antlers (bones at the top of their head). Male deer use their antlers to fight rivals and they grow a new set every year.

The Cardamom Mountains are also home to the largest wild Asian elephant population in Southeast Asia. Their huge, round footprints can be seen in the mud of the elephant corridor—a track that many elephants use to travel through the jungle.

Asian elephants can grow up to 13 feet tall and have a diet of grass, fruit, leaves, and bark. An elephant's trunk is an extension of its nose and upper lip and can be used to break off branches and leaves, and feed them into its mouth to eat. Elephant trunks also come in handy for sucking up water for the elephant to drink or throw over its body to keep it cool.

Growing to such huge sizes, elephants are incredibly heavy. If scientists are lucky enough to encounter them, they will probably hear them crashing through the jungle before they see them. They just need to make sure they keep out of the elephants' way—despite their large size, charging elephants can move with surprising speed.

Tigers are the biggest and strongest cats in the world. Known for their ferocity, they will eat deer, and many other animals, for breakfast. Seeing their round, yellow eyes and sharp, pointed teeth glinting in the undergrowth is enough to bring terror to any jungle creature.

Tigers know when to stay quiet, and their silence and stealth make them skilled hunters. However, their loud roar can send the birds scattering from the treetops. Tigers, lions, jaguars, and leopards are the only cats that can roar—they are all called "big cats."

The telltale sign of a tiger lurking in trees is the flash of its distinctive stripes. These markings on the tiger's coat blend in with the shadows so that it can creep closer to its prey before jumping in for the kill. Each tiger's stripes are unique, just like human fingerprints.

Tigers have super sharp senses, which

allow them to do most of their hunting at nighttime. They can see six times better than humans in dim light and their eyes appear to glow in the dark because they reflect any light that shines on them.

Just like any domestic cat, tigers have whiskers to help them feel their way around. Unlike their domestic cousins, however, wild tigers can grow to an intimidating 10 feet long.

Although tigers may look cuddly, they are anything but. Male tigers have a strong territorial nature and will fight to the death to protect their home and mate. A female tiger is called a tigress and can have many cubs throughout her lifetime. These cubs will stay with her for 2 to 3 years until they can hunt for themselves.

Apart from a mother and her cubs, most tigers are solitary creatures that live and hunt alone. However, tigers can identify

each other from their smell or even from the scratches that they leave on trees.

Although tigers are not threatened by any other jungle animals, there is one creature that they can't protect themselves against—humans. Their fur can fetch high prices, making tigers very attractive targets for hunters. The research of mammalogists is crucial to try and stop this from happening. Their findings help people understand tigers and seek ways of preserving their species and increasing their numbers in the wild.

Tiger Fact File

Tigers are the largest cats in the world. They are endangered, which means that there are very few of them left in the wild. The two biggest threats to tigers are hunting and deforestation—both caused by humans. There are now only about 3,200 tigers living in the wild.

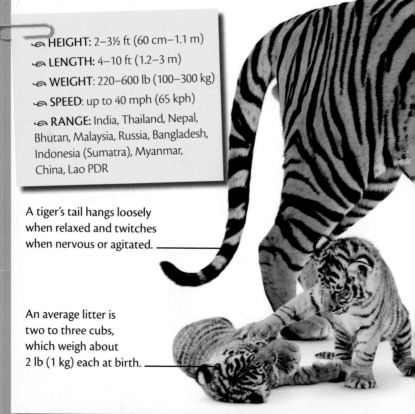

- **HEIGHT:** 2–3½ ft (60 cm–1.1 m)
- **LENGTH:** 4–10 ft (1.2–3 m)
- **WEIGHT:** 220–600 lb (100–300 kg)
- **SPEED:** up to 40 mph (65 kph)
- **RANGE:** India, Thailand, Nepal, Bhutan, Malaysia, Russia, Bangladesh, Indonesia (Sumatra), Myanmar, China, Lao PDR

A tiger's tail hangs loosely when relaxed and twitches when nervous or agitated. _____

An average litter is two to three cubs, which weigh about 2 lb (1 kg) each at birth. _____

TIGERS LIKE WATER AND OFTEN SWIM IN POOLS TO COOL OFF.

No two tigers have the same pattern of stripes.

Tigers hunt at night; they can see well in the dark.

A tiger's roar can be heard up to 2 miles (3 km) away.

Tigers sneak up on their prey and then pounce using their teeth and claws to pull the animal down.

Nocturnal Animals

SLOW LORIS ❯

This loris gets its name from its slow speed. Lorises have gripping hands that are great for climbing through trees, and big eyes so they can see at night easily.

❮ PALM CIVET

Striped, bushy-tailed palm civets are able to live in a range of habitats. They mostly live in trees but sometimes look for mice and insects on the ground.

YELLOW-THROATED MARTEN ❯

These brightly colored animals have very long tails and eat fruit and small animals. They are not shy and are known for their unpleasant smell.

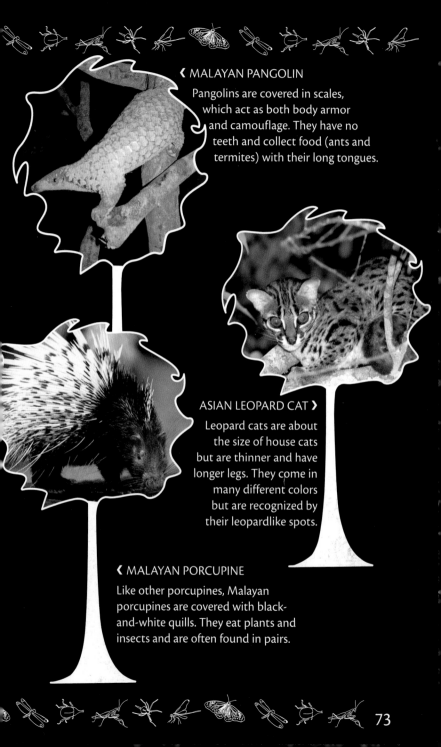

❮ MALAYAN PANGOLIN

Pangolins are covered in scales, which act as both body armor and camouflage. They have no teeth and collect food (ants and termites) with their long tongues.

ASIAN LEOPARD CAT ❯

Leopard cats are about the size of house cats but are thinner and have longer legs. They come in many different colors but are recognized by their leopardlike spots.

❮ MALAYAN PORCUPINE

Like other porcupines, Malayan porcupines are covered with black-and-white quills. They eat plants and insects and are often found in pairs.

CHAPTER 5
Bugs, Bugs, Bugs!

Collecting creepy-crawlers has been the career of choice for many people, dating back more than three centuries. This has made it possible for scientists to identify most of the minibeasts living in Europe. However, many of the species living in the tropics still remain a mystery.

Scientists are often interested in how insects help mantain the delicate balance of nature—how they pollinate flowers and trees and provide nutrients for other plants and animals in the jungle.

Scientists who study insects are called entomologists, and those who study arachnids (spiders, ticks, and scorpions) are called arachnologists. Spiders are different from insects because they have eight legs and two body parts, whereas insects have three pairs of legs and three body sections.

Entomologists and arachnologists need to be the most eagle-eyed of all scientists because the animals they study are so tiny—many insect species measure less than 0.04 inches long! Once they have caught the miniscule critters, the scientists will often need to use a magnifying glass or microscope to examine and identify them.

When hiking through the jungle, explorers will often have the unpleasant experience of accidentally walking through a spider's web. These expertly created, sticky strands can hold 4,000 times the spider's own weight and are used to catch insects for the spider to eat.

Some spiders spin their webs and then lie in wait until insects land on it. Hairs on their legs detect movement on the web so they know when to leap out and pounce on their prey. Once caught, spiders will inject their prey with poison to paralyze them, and will often wrap them in silky cocoons to make them easier to transport back to their lairs.

As hunters, spiders are very important to the jungle ecosystem. On average, a spider will eat 2,000 insects a year, which helps stop the insect population getting out of control.

Some species of spiders can grow as large as 9 inches and have adapted to be able to jump long distances. Jumping can help them catch prey, but can also help them avoid getting eaten by other animals. To hide from predators some spiders can camouflage themselves. The Hersilia spider, which lives in the Cardamoms, has markings on its body that perfectly mimic a certain type of lichen. This makes it almost impossible to spot when it is lying flat against a tree trunk.

Another jungle animal that is very good at camouflaging itself is the praying mantis. The common mantis has a green or brown coloring to help it blend into the foliage in its habitat. Like many other insects, its wings resemble leaves and it has adapted to be a highly specialized predator. Its front legs have sharp barbs or spines to help it grasp and hold its prey while eating. These front legs give the insect its name—the way that they are bent makes it look as though it is praying.

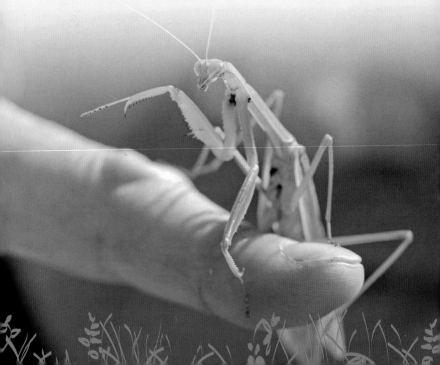

Although it does have wings, the praying mantis rarely uses them, except for when it needs to fly and escape predators. The Cardamom Mountains however does have a lot of insect air traffic, and it is impossible to avoid the flies that are constantly flitting around in the dappled sunlight.

The thrumming of the flies' wings, the chirping of the crickets, and the buzzing of the bees can cause quite a racket at times and explorers are reminded of all the tiny creatures riding the airwaves.

Honeybees are one of the world's most useful insects, providing honey and wax and also helping to pollinate plants. Pollination is when pollen is transferred from the male to the female parts of a plant. This allows the female parts to reproduce and create seeds, which will then grow into new plants. Many insects help in this process.

During the daytime in the jungle, scientists can expect to see flashes of color darting through the trees. These will be the numerous, brightly patterned butterflies that live there. The most exotic species of butterflies live in warm tropical areas and have such vibrant wings to help them attract a mate and to warn other animals not to eat them.

When the sun sets and the butterflies settle down for the night, the moths come out. Being nocturnal, moths' wings have more muted and earthy tones than butterflies' wings. Another way of telling them apart is that moths tend to rest their wings flat, whereas butterflies hold their wings upright.

The life cycle of butterflies and moths consists of four different stages: egg, caterpillar, pupa, and adult. As soon as they emerge from their eggs, caterpillars are greedy little grubs. Some are such quick

eaters that, if there are too many of them, they can quickly strip a tree of all its leaves!

As adults, butterflies and moths feed on plant nectar and other liquids. They use a long, hollow feeding tube, called a proboscis, to suck these up.

Surprisingly, catching insects in the jungle can be easier than tracking some of the larger animals. Entomologists can use a technique called canopy fogging to catch lots of little creatures at once.

Scientists will put the fogger high up in the trees and then arrange some funnel-shaped containers on the ground below. The fogger is remote controlled and when it is turned on, it releases a chemical that confuses any insects or arachnids in the surrounding tree. In this confused state, the creatures won't be able to hold on to the tree or their webs, and they will rain down from the branches and into the funnels.

Once there, the scientists can record what species they are, what they look like, and how many there are of each type of creature. The bugs' bodies are tough and are able to handle the impact of the fall. The effects of the chemical are only temporary and once they have worn off, the creatures will just carry on with their business, as if nothing happened.

Hide and Seek

Insects are all around us, but many are so well camouflaged that they are hard to spot. With the help of a tray and a piece of white paper, you can bring them out into the open.

WHAT YOU WILL NEED:
shallow tray
white paper
scissors
stick
magnifying glass

WARNING!
Always ask an adult for help when using sharp scissors.

1 Cut a piece of white paper to fit the bottom of your tray. Line the tray with the paper.

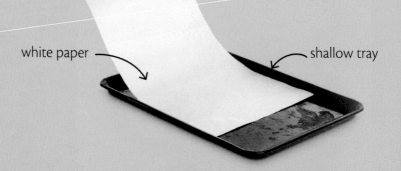

white paper

shallow tray

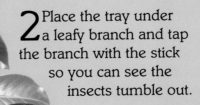

2 Place the tray under a leafy branch and tap the branch with the stick so you can see the insects tumble out.

magnifying glass

3 Use the magnifying glass to get a close-up view of the insects as they fly or crawl away. Try using the tray under different plants to see which bugs live where.

IMPORTANT: Do not pick up any of the bugs you collect because they may bite or sting—or you might hurt them! Let them crawl or fly back to where they came from.

85

CHAPTER 6
Reptile Rescue

Croaking, hissing, slithering, and jumping through the jungle are lots of exciting species of reptiles and amphibians. The scientists who are fanatical about frogs and inspired by snakes are called herpetologists and the Cardamom Mountains is the perfect place to find their slippery specimens.

There are about 2,700 species of snakes in the world and they all thrive in warm climates. Snakes come in all shapes and sizes—some are small enough to fit into the palm of your hand, but others, such as

pythons, can grow up to 23 feet long!

All snakes eat meat and swallow their prey whole. This is because their teeth are not strong enough to grind up their food. Most species of snake are not venomous and so pose no threat to humans. However some do have poisonous liquid in their fangs that they can use to stun their victims before devouring them. Some snakes, like this young vine snake, live high in the treetops and disguise themselves as vines. Others squirm around on the jungle floor or glide through the rivers nearby.

Amphibians are animals such as frogs, and salamanders, that can live both on land and in water.

When moving around on land, frogs are great climbers that are able to cling onto even the smoothest of surfaces. The sticky, mucus-filled pads on the end of each of their toes gives them a firm grip on any surface.

When swimming in the water, frogs can also dart around with ease. Frogs start their lives as frogspawn (jellylike eggs in the water) and learn how to swim as soon as they transform into tiny tadpoles. Once fully grown, frogs are expert swimmers—their technique is very similar to the breaststroke that humans use.

Frogs lack weapons such as claws or teeth, which they could use to defend themselves against predators. Instead they rely on their strong back legs to help them jump out of harm's way. Some frogs can produce liquids from the glands in their skin which make them taste bad to other animals. In some cases, these liquids can be poisonous and can even kill their predators. Posionous frogs are usually the most brightly colored and many of them are usually found in the Cardamoms.

How are frogs able to be good climbers?

The Cardamom Mountains is home to one of the most endangered crocodile species in the world. Siamese crocodiles were thought to be completely extinct until recent years, when they were rediscovered in Cambodia.

These elusive creatures live in the slow-moving rivers in the jungle and are gentle animals, despite their tough exterior. There are thought to be fewer than 5,000 individuals left in the wild—perhaps even as few as 250.

Very little is known about the Siamese crocodile, which is why it is so important for scientists to travel to Cambodia and discover more about it.

Crocodiles belong to a group of animals called crocodilians, which also includes alligators, caimans, and gharials. Crocodilians are some of the few survivors from the time of the dinosaurs, which was approximately 250 million years ago, and have changed very little in this time.

Crocodiles are semiaquatic predators and they're not fussy about what they eat, be it live animals or those that are already dead.

When stalking prey, crocodiles calmly float along the river, waiting for the right moment to jump up and bare their ferocious jaws. Crocodiles are so well camouflaged that when they are submerged, animals will often mistake them for pieces of driftwood bobbing in the river current. Once they are close enough, crocodiles surprise their prey and grab and crush it in their jaws. They will drag their victim down under the water's surface to

drown it. After their meal has successfully been caught, crocodiles sometimes hide the body under the riverbank, to be eaten as a tasty snack at a later time.

Although crocodile jaws are incredibly powerful, they can also be used for more delicate work. When hatchlings (baby crocodiles that have just emerged from their eggs) are ready to swim, their mother will transport them from the nest and into the water in her mouth. This shows great tenderness and care. Maybe they are just big scaly softies after all!

Crocodiles, frogs, fish, and other aquatic animals all live in the Prek Tnort River, which flows into the great Mekong River. According to legend, the great Naga— a giant, snakelike creature—lives in the Mekong. Some years back, they discovered a new species of giant catfish living in the river—at nearly 10 feet long, it really was a whopper! Some people think that this must be where the stories came from, but others like to believe that the mystical Naga is still out there.

Although this fish was once found in abundance in the Mekong, its population numbers have seriously dwindled in recent years. Primarily due to overfishing, this giant fish is now critically endangered.

Mekong giant catfish are docile creatures and are toothless herbivores, who survive off the plants and algae in the river.

Catfish are named for the catlike whiskers, or "barbels," that the young have near their

mouths. Barbels are covered in taste buds that help the fish find food, but these features shrink as the fish gets older.

Catfish and their relatives account for three quarters of all species of freshwater fish, however, like many other animals in the jungle, they still need the help of humans to continue thriving in the wild.

THE MYSTERIOUS NAGA

BORN FROM THE NAGA

Cambodians sometimes say that they are "born from the Naga." In Cambodian legend, the Naga were a race of reptiles, and the Cambodian people are descendants of the marriage between the Naga king's daughter and the king of ancient Cambodia.

NAGA SYMBOL

Naga are familiar symbols in many Southeast Asian countries. They symbolize prosperity and the spirit of the land and water. In Cambodia, Naga often appear on temples and bridges.

GIANT CATFISH OF THE MEKONG

Perhaps the legendary Naga are really giant catfish. The Mekong River is known to be home to the Mekong giant catfish, the largest freshwater fish in the world, weighing as much as 750 lbs (340 kg) and measuring up to 10 ft (3 m) in length.

NAGA FIREBALLS

Every year during the bright full moon in the fall, mysterious fireballs shoot up from the Mekong River into the sky above. Scientists have been unable to find a logical explanation. Legend has it that the Naga spit these fireballs to celebrate the end of the fall rains. Could the legend be true?

CARDAMOM DISPATCHES

ABOUT ME

My name's Charlotte, and I'm a student training to become a biologist. I decided to join my mentor Liz on a scientific expedition to the Cardamom Mountains of Cambodia. This is my blog about it. My likes include sleeping, fashion, and, most of all, animals (especially big cats)!

DAY 20
September 28
CARDAMOM MOUNTAINS

There's never a dull moment in the Cardamom Mountains. Our expedition team flew in by helicopter and we had to make an emergency landing. We've hiked through the jungle and seen spectacular and beautiful plants and animals. I had a snake in my boot and one of our team broke her leg and had to be evacuated out of the jungle! I didn't think our expedition could get any more exciting, but wait until I tell you what happened next.

Liz was desperate to find a Siamese crocodile, so she and I headed upriver to observe the animals that live in and near the water. We saw a lot of amazing creatures—lots of different frogs and fish, including bullfrogs and catfish. While we were eating lunch, I noticed that the water was turning a darker color and that there were lots of leaves and branches in it. That's when we realized—it was a flash flood! We made it to a safe place on top of a hill just in time. It really was close!

The flood meant that we didn't manage to see the crocodile. We did see something else, though: on another hill nearby, I saw the last thing I expected to see—a tiger! He was just lying down on a big rock, as if nothing was happening! He was so beautiful.

Before coming on the expedition, I had really hoped I would get to see a tiger. I knew I might not because tigers are extremely rare, but now I have had three sightings! I wonder if all three are the same tiger. I feel so lucky. This trip's turning out to be such an amazing experience. I can't wait to see what happens next!

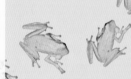

CHAPTER 7
Helping the Jungle

Before the time of humans, animals and plants in the jungle only needed to protect themselves against each other. But in recent years, humans have learned that there are many ways that they can exploit the resources of the jungle. In 2002, a large freeway was built through the Cardamom Mountains, which opened the area up to more people. Many of these people use the area for farming but are still very poor.

Many farmers use a technique called slash-and-burn. When farmers need to clear land to grow crops, they cut down all the trees and burn whatever's left—branches, leaves, stumps, and even the tree trunks. It makes the ground fertile in the short term, but it's extremely harmful to the jungle, the animals that live in it, and the air around it.

This approach can permanently damage the soil so that new trees cannot grow.

Wildlife associations have been trying to target these farmers and help them find more sustainable ways of clearing land and growing crops. This has been successful in many areas and people have been able to grow more crops and make more money as well as looking after the environment.

With the help of the local people and conservation organizations, the impact that humans have on the Cardamom Mountains is slowly being brought under control. However, the natural world isn't so easy to manage, and the Cambodian climate can wreak havoc on the habitats of both animals and humans.

The large amount of rain that the jungle experiences makes the area prone to flash flooding. This is where an area will flood very quickly, often following heavy rainfall. Animals and humans can get swept along with the water and may even drown. If scientists are in the jungle during a flash flood, they need to act quickly and move to higher ground. They may have to wait for hours until the water eases and they can return to their camp.

During a flash flood the river water will become frothy and turn brownish in color, and will wash mud, leaves, branches, and animals down to other parts of the jungle. The strong waters can also destroy the crops and rice fields that many farmers depend on to make a living. Cambodia is one of the world's largest exporters of rice so the loss of fields can have devastating effects. Many people still struggle to make enough money to support their families and some have to turn to more dangerous and illegal ways to do so.

Wildlife poaching is one of the major causes of animal death in the Cardamoms. Cambodia is home to 14 of the world's most endangered species, including the Malaysian sun bear, Asian elephant, Indochinese tiger, and the pileated gibbon.

People from rural communities see these animals as a way to make money quickly. They trap and kill the animals and sell them. Ultimately, however, it is actually the powerful people they work for who benefit the most.

Underprivileged people find poaching attractive because it offers Cambodian

farmers the opportuntity to make 250 times their usual monthly salary from the sale of just one tiger. Elephant tusks alone can fetch up to $15,000 on the black market.

Poaching of endangered animals is illegal and scientists, jungle rangers, and Buddhist monks have all joined forces to try and stop animals being killed for their meat, fur, and ivory. It is an uphill battle and many of the animals that get caught in poachers' snares are no longer able to survive in the wild.

Wildlife centers, such as the Phnom Tamao Wildlife Rescue Center near Phnom Peng, take in injured animals and cares for them until they are well enough to be released into the wild. If the animals do not make a full recovery, then the center will

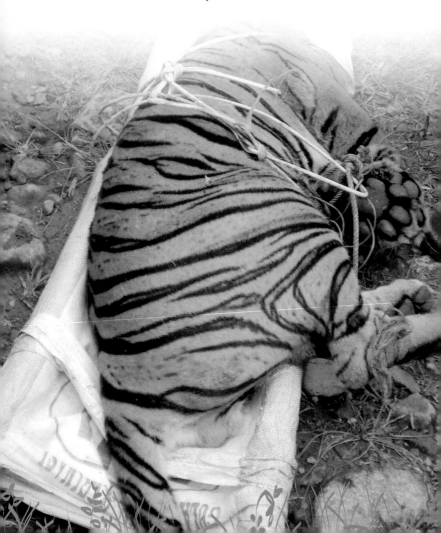

find a new and safe home for them.

However, if an animal's habitat disappears they cannot be released back into the wild. This is one of the problems caused by deforestation. Every second an area of jungle the size of a soccer field disappears. If this continues, by 2060 there will be none left. The demand for farmland, wood, and biofuels (fuel made from crops) has increased the amount of illegal logging in jungle areas. Illegal logging is not done in a sustainable way like selective logging, so it is impossible to control the rate at which the trees are cut down.

Selective logging means that only certain trees are cut down, rather than whole areas being cleared at once. Sunlight can then reach the forest floor, which encourages the growth of new trees. This is one of the many solutions that is encouraged in the Cardamoms, to try to save the jungle.

Protecting the jungle is not easy but many people work hard to educate others and reduce the impact that humans have on this habitat. The important research that is carried out by field scientists means that we now have a greater understanding of the creatures and plants that inhabit the jungle. Since transportation links in jungle areas

are becoming more sophisticated, more people are able to visit and learn about the jungle first-hand. A new kind of responsible travel, called ecotourism, is encouraged in places such as the Cardamom Mountains. Ecotourists can visit natural areas to sightsee or learn about the environment without staying in a fancy hotel or using up valuable resources. Visitor numbers are limited and care is taken not to upset the delicate ecosystem of the jungle. Tourists bring money to the area that can be used for important conservation work.

The jungle is a bountiful resource that may hold the answers to many questions about life on Earth. Protecting it is as important to the animals living there as it is to humans who live on the other side of the planet. The combined effort of charities, scientists, monks, and locals will help preserve jungles so that they can be enjoyed for years to come.

Global Warming and Deforestation

Destroying forests has a major impact on our planet. Studying the diversity of animals in a given area (its biodiversity) provides clues as to how the planet is doing. This chart shows what can happen if forests are destroyed.

HUMANS CUT AND BURN DOWN TREES TO USE THE TIMBER OR TO CLEAR THE LAND FOR FARMING.

THERE ARE NOT ENOUGH TREES TO PROCESS THE CARBON DIOXIDE (CO_2) EMITTED BY ANIMALS AND HUMANS.

CO_2 IN THE AIR INCREASES.

ANIMALS ARE FORCED TO MOVE AWAY FROM THEIR NATURAL HABITATS.

ANIMAL ATTACKS ON HUMANS INCREASE.

ANIMALS START MOVING INTO AREAS WHERE HUMANS LIVE.

THE SUN'S LIGHT BECOMES TRAPPED IN THE ATMOSPHERE MORE EASILY, CAUSING GLOBAL TEMPERATURES TO INCREASE.

WEATHER PATTERNS CHANGE.

EXTREME WEATHER, SUCH AS BLIZZARDS, DROUGHTS, AND HURRICANES, BECOMES WIDESPREAD.

POLAR ICE CAPS MELT, AND SEA LEVEL RISES.

FLOODING BECOMES MORE COMMON, AND THERE IS THE POSSIBILITY THAT COASTAL COMMUNITIES MAY BE DESTROYED BY THE SEA.

ANIMALS HAVE TROUBLE FINDING FOOD AND MIGHT STARVE.

SPECIES BECOME EXTINCT.

Welcome to Phnom Tamao Wildlife Rescue Center

The Phnom Tamao Wildlife Rescue Center is run by the Cambodian Forestry Administration, with support from the Wildlife Alliance, an organization that aims to protect wildlife and their habitats. At Phnom Tamao, more than 1,200 rescued animals are cared for, and ultimately returned to the wild if possible. No animal in need is ever turned away.

Chhouk's story

Chhouk, a young Asian elephant, has a prosthetic foot. He was found as a baby, wandering the forest alone. He had lost his foot in a poacher's snare, and the wound was infected. Wildlife Alliance cared for him in the forest for two weeks, before transporting him to Phnom Tamao. Chhouk is now healthy again and walks around on his prosthetic foot as if nothing happened.

Meet the animals

Phnom Tamao is home to a range of animals who will be happy to welcome you. Come and meet them!

How You Can Help

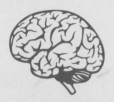

BE INFORMED

Find out as much as you can about endangered animals and their habitats. If you are well informed, you can better spread the message to others that endangered animals need our help.

HELP CONSERVATION ORGANIZATIONS

Sponsor an animal through a wildlife organization, such as Wildlife Alliance (www.wildlifealliance.org), or protect an acre of land through Conservation International (www. conservation.org), which has helped protect the Cardamoms since 2002. Donations will support conservation of the forests and species like the ones described in this book.

There are many ways to help look after animals and the forests. Here is how to get started.

GO GREEN

Help prevent climate change. Reduce the amount of greenhouse gases, such as carbon dioxide, that is released into the air as a result of the things people do. Reuse, repair, or recycle things instead of throwing them away. Save energy by turning off electricity when it is not needed. Walk, bike, or take public transportation instead of the car.

PROTECT FORESTS

Buy wood products certified by the Forest Stewardship Council (FSC). This means that the wood is from forests that are carefully looked after to prevent losing too many trees or harming wildlife or local communities.

TIGERS

If you love tigers, find out more about how to save them at Save Tigers Now (www.savetigersnow.org).

Meet the Experts

PEPPER WILDE: Hello! And welcome to Meet the Experts. I'm Pepper Wilde. Today we're speaking to three scientists who've just returned from an expedition counting the animals in the Cardamom Mountains of Cambodia—Liz Terrapin, Anthony Bugg, and Phrun Keo. Welcome!

LIZ TERRAPIN: Thank you for having us.

PW: So, why exactly were you counting the animals?

LT: By counting the animals, we can see whether any of them are in danger of extinction, whether those that were endangered aren't anymore, and if there are any new species we need to start looking after. All of this helps us plan how we can help animals. It also tells us how our planet as a whole is doing because animals are the first ones to know when something isn't right with the Earth.

PW: What made you decide to do the survey in Cambodia?

ANTHONY BUGG: The Cardamom Mountains are rich with rare wildlife, much of it endemic, meaning that it only exists here. This is also an area that has not been explored much and needs to be studied.

PW: What was it like out there?

LT: Amazing and beautiful. It's so peaceful. There are no other people, just lots of fantastic animals—birds, butterflies, lizards, snakes, frogs, monkeys...

PHRUN KEO: It's really hot and humid, too! You're sweating all the time. It's definitely an adventure, though—full of surprises!

PW: What was the best part of the trip for you?

LT: Seeing a species I hadn't seen before! People are discovering new species in the Cardamoms all the time, but it was still a big thrill for me!

PK: For me, it was getting some awesome pictures from my camera trap. Camera traps are a great way to capture photos of animals because there are no people around to scare them away. Animals just act normally, so we got some fantastic pictures of porcupines, deer, and a tiger.

PW: Would you do it all again?

LT: Definitely!

AB: Absolutely!

PK: In a heartbeat!

Jungle Quiz

See if you can remember the answers to these questions about what you have read.

1. What is the name for scientists who study fish?

2. What is a biodiversity study?

3. What is the name of the highest mountain in Cambodia?

4. What is the capital city of Cambodia called?

5. Which reptile was discovered in the Cardamom Mountains in 2000?

6. Which kingdom of living things do humans belong to?

7. What should you do if you get bitten by a leech?

8. What is the top layer of jungle trees called?

9. What is the name for the group of animals that feed on dead leaves and plant debris?

10. How are monkeys different from apes?

11. True or false: every tiger's stripes are different.

12. What are baby tigers called?

13. What is the name given to the group of animals that live on land and in water?

14. Which real-life animal might be the legendary Naga?

15. What technique do people living near the Cardamom Mountains use to clear land?

Answers on page 121.

Glossary

Adapt
Adjust to new conditions.

Boisterous
Noisy and energetic.

Climate
Weather conditions in a certain area.

Dehydration
When the body doesn't have enough water.

Docile
Laid-back and gentle.

Ecosystem
A community of plants and animals that interact and rely upon each other.

Fertile
Able to grow many healthy crops.

Flora
Plants of a particular region or habitat.

Herbivore
An animal that only eats plants.

Humidity
Amount of water in the air.

Intrepid
Adventurous and unafraid.

Lichen
Mosslike plant found on rocks or trees.

Logging
Activity of cutting down trees.

Machete
A knife used for cutting large plants.

Nocturnal
Active at night.

Predator
Animal that hunts and eats other animals.

Rejuvenate
Give new strength or energy to something.

Semiaquatic
Living partly on land and partly on water.

Sustainable
Using something at a manageable rate so that it does not run out too quickly.

Tropics
Region of Earth surrounding the equator.

Answers to the Jungle Quiz:
1. Ichthyologists; **2.** When scientists count how many of each type of animal they can find in an area; **3.** Mount Aural; **4.** Phnom Penh; **5.** The Cardamom Mountains wolf snake; **6.** Animals; **7.** Leave it alone until it drops off; **8.** The emergent layer; **9.** Decomposers; **10.** Monkeys have tails; **11.** True; **12.** Cubs; **13.** Amphibians; **14.** The Mekong giant catfish; **15.** Slash-and-burn farming.

Index

About the Author

Katy Lennon was born and raised in the UK where she spent her childhood reading as many books as she could get her hands on. She moved to the seaside town of Brighton to study for her degree in English Literature and Media Studies, and now enjoys being an editor at DK, helping to create books for young, inquiring minds. She lives in East London with three housemates and two cats and spends her spare time knitting, watching films, reading, and listening to records on her Dad's old record player.

About the Consultant

Dr. Linda Gambrell, Distinguished Professor of Education at Clemson University, has served as President of the National Reading Conference, the College Reading Association, and the International Reading Association. She is also reading consultant to the *DK Readers*.

Have you read these other great books from DK?

DK ADVENTURES

Discover the wonders of the world's deepest, darkest ocean trench.

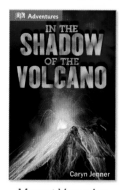

Mount Vesuvius erupts in this adventure. Will Carlo escape?

It's a life-or-death adventure as the gang searches for a new home planet.

Chase twisters in Tornado Alley in this pulse-racing action adventure.

Discover what life for pilots, women, and children was like during WWII.

Emma adores horses. Will her wish come true at a riding camp?

Have you read these other great books from DK?

DK ADVENTURES

Lucy follows her dream… Will she make the cut?

Experience ancient Roman intrigue in this time-traveling adventure.

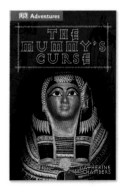

Experience ancient Egyptian life… Are our time-travelers cursed?

Time-travel to the Wild West and get caught up in fossil hunters' rivalry.

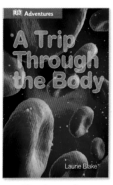

Explore the amazing systems at work inside the human body.

Step back nearly 20,000 years to the days of early cave dwellers.